FAMILY CARS OF
THE 1970s

James Taylor

SHIRE PUBLICATIONS

Published in Great Britain in 2012 by Shire Publications Ltd, Midland House, West Way, Botley, Oxford OX2 0PH, United Kingdom.

44-02 23rd Street, Suite 219, Long Island City, NY 11101, USA.

E-mail: shire@shirebooks.co.uk   www.shirebooks.co.uk

© 2012 James Taylor.

A CIP catalogue record for this book is available from the British Library.

Shire Library no. 688.   ISBN-13: 978 0 74781 149 7

James Taylor has asserted his right under the Copyright, Designs and Patents Act, 1988, to be identified as the author of this book.

Designed by Tony Truscott Designs, Sussex, UK and typeset in Perpetua and Gill Sans.

Printed in China through Worldprint Ltd.

12 13 14 15 16   10 9 8 7 6 5 4 3 2 1

COVER IMAGE
A Triumph Toledo, one of the more upmarket family saloons.

TITLE PAGE IMAGE
The MkIII Cortina was emblematic of 1970s Britain. The 'Coca-Cola bottle' styling was a classic that still looks good today, even though the car was mechanically ordinary. This is a top-specification GXL model, with the ubiquitous vinyl roof.

CONTENTS PAGE IMAGE
The Alfasud was the shape of things to come. Nimble, and great fun to drive, it lacked only a hatchback and effective rustproofing to have been a truly great car.

ACKNOWLEDGEMENTS
Illustrations are acknowledged as follows:

Alamy, pages 3 and 4; BMW, page 26 (both); Coventry Transport Museum, pages 32 (bottom), 33 (both), 34, and 35 (both); Fiat, pages 44 (top) and 45; Ford Motor Co, pages 1, 6, 14, 15, 16, 17 (both), 18, and 19 (both); GM-Opel, page 48 (both); GM-Vauxhall, pages 20 (both), 21, 22 (all), and 23; Nissan, pages 58 and 59; PSA Peugeot-Citroën, pages 38 (bottom), 39 (all), and 40 (all); Dave Richards, pages 55 (both), and 56 (centre and bottom); Saab, page 46; Volvo, page 53 (both); VW-Audi, pages 49 (both), 50 (both), 51 (both), and 52 (both).

Shire Publications is supporting the Woodland Trust, the UK's leading woodland conservation charity, by funding the dedication of trees.

CONTENTS

The Maxi is no ordinary car. It's a very comfortable five seater saloon when you want a saloon.

In fact, it's a lot more comfortable than most, with standard features like fully adjustable and reclining front seats and fitted carpeting throughout.

The Maxi is an estate when you want an estate. Simply fold the rear seats forward and there's 44·5 cu. ft. of load space behind you.

The Maxi combines fast lane motorway performance (the fifth gear keeps the revs. and petrol consumption down) with rally class roadholding – front wheel drive and radial tyres keep it firmly on the road.

The Maxi does so much more.

Your life is full of surprising variety. Your car should be the same.

From British Leyland.
Makers of the best selling cars in Britain.

Maxi. It goes with a way of life.

PREFACE

IT HAS BECOME FASHIONABLE to deride the cars of the 1970s as unappealing, unexciting and poorly built. Many certainly were. This was the period when Britain's domestic motor industry, or at least that large part of it which belonged to the British Leyland empire, hit such a crisis that it was nationalised in a hurry during 1975 to prevent thousands of men and women being put out of work. Tellingly, perhaps, this was also the period when interest in older, 'classic' cars began to increase dramatically, and many of those who became involved at the time would argue that the interest was aroused precisely because the latest crop of new cars was indeed unappealing, unexciting and poorly built.

With the benefit of hindsight, however, the 1970s was a very interesting decade for cars, and particularly so for family cars, the subject of this book. Family cars, by definition, are likely to be less appealing to traditional car enthusiasts. Rather than high-performance supercars or even affordable sports models, they tend to be saloons and estates designed for primarily practical purposes. They are built to sell at a moderate price, too, although the upper limit for family saloons jumped from £1,500 at the start of the 1970s to £5,000 by the end of the decade, in line with inflation.

But these are the cars that people remember: they knew them well because their parents, uncles and grandparents had them. These are the cars that took them to school (even though little faces pressed against steamed-up windows may have been more interested in the very occasional Ferrari that roared into view). The quirks, the smells and the foibles of those cars remain indelibly imprinted on the minds of those who knew them so well. More than just cars, they were part of the social fabric of 1970s Britain.

So this book looks at some of the key models that were available to family buyers during the 1970s. It looks at both British and imported models, but rarely strays outside the realm of the cars that Dad bought (for he still made such decisions in the 1970s). He may have dreamed of a Jaguar or Mercedes, but they were beyond his reach. Instead, he bought a Hillman Avenger, a Renault 12 or a Chrysler Horizon. They were the cars of the 1970s and, for many families, they provided dependable and even characterful transport.

Opposite:
The Austin Maxi was practical and versatile but somehow was more memorable for its odd looks and questionable gearchange.

5

INTRODUCTION

FAMILY MOTORING in 1970s Britain was an established phenomenon. Although roads were not as congested as they have since become, and travel by bus, coach or train was still a part of everyday life for most families, car ownership had become the family norm.

Motoring in the 1970s was set against a background of Green Shield stamps with every gallon of petrol, and against alarming increases in the cost of that petrol after the two oil crises in 1973 and 1979. Edward Heath's government issued petrol-ration coupons at the end of 1973 in case fuel supplies became scarce, and for a time the motorway speed limit was restricted to 55 mph. Before the 1970s, the amount of petrol that a car consumed was probably of little concern to a majority of users, but as prices increased during the decade there was a new focus on miles per gallon as a factor in evaluating a car's desirability.

The 1970s in Britain were also characterised by seemingly perpetual strikes in the domestic motor industry. Rightly or wrongly, union convenors whipped up fervour against the cutbacks and reorganisations that were necessary to lick an already ailing industry into some sort of fighting trim. Against such a background, it was something of a miracle that the British motor industry managed to produce anything at all, let alone to come up with new models fairly regularly.

Of course, all these problems took their toll. Foreign manufacturers, especially in Europe and Japan, saw a car-buying populace that was disappointed in the products of domestic manufacturers and quite often had to wait for unacceptably long periods before its new-car orders were fulfilled. So the 1970s in Britain were characterised by an unprecedented influx of cars from abroad. Many were good; some were no better than the domestic product; but they were at least available on demand, and with a smile from the local salesman.

Car manufacturers still exhibited national characteristics, and the time of the 'global' design had not yet come. Though frequently bordering on caricature, popular opinions of cars imported into Britain tended to be

Opposite:
Ford cars – an Escort estate and the front of a Granada estate – form the backdrop as designer Hardy Amies shows off his 1973 fashion collection in London. Just behind the Escort is a Volvo 144, a sign that foreign manufacturers were gaining a new foothold in the British family car market.

7

remarkably accurate. Italian cars were noisy, sporty and rusted quickly; French cars had quirky designs but were good family holdalls; German cars were expensive but well made; Eastern European and Russian cars were cheap but not very cheerful; Swedish cars were solid, sensible and safe. As for the Japanese, their designs were simply odd, their engineering out of date, but their build quality admirable.

By and large, British buyers still wanted to buy British cars. But there were so many good foreign models available, and the quality of the domestic product was so variable, that family buyers tended to go for the safe option. They bought imported cars, and the health of the British motor industry went from bad to worse as a result. In 1975, imported cars still accounted for only 33 per cent of all new cars sold through British showrooms. By the end of the decade, imports were accounting for well over 50 per cent of all new car sales, and the balance was tilting increasingly rapidly away from British manufacturers.

Meanwhile, the design of the family car itself was changing. As the decade opened, the typical family car was a four-door saloon with four or five seats, with the 'three-box' configuration of a bonnet and boot projecting from the front and rear of the passenger cabin. It had a longitudinally mounted petrol engine of between 900cc and about 2 litres that drove the rear wheels through a four-speed manual gearbox.

Ten years later, the engine of the typical family car was likely to be mounted transversely and to be driving the front wheels. Many cars had a 'two-box' design with no separate projecting boot, but rather a sloping hatchback that gave access to a luggage compartment in the tail. More cars had automatic gearboxes, and most incorporated more safety features and used less fuel. The first diesel engines were appearing in Britain – although they had long been popular on the European mainland. Styling fashion, too, was changing, as more angular shapes replaced the comfortable rotundity of the 1960s designs.

Popular colours – for British-built cars at least – included several shades of beige and fawn, plus a few dark browns for good measure. At the other end of the colour spectrum, bright yellows and lime greens

Why you can see through our latest efforts to make you a better driver.

"SMITHS" extra-wide 30" Rear Window Heater: It covers more window to uncover more window. A full 30" × 9½", so that even on the widest wrap-round window, every square inch can be kept clear and mist-free. Well designed, but nothing to look at. Actually, it's nothing to look at *because* it's so well designed.

Unlike some rear window heaters, there's no distorting plastic to obscure the view, and no air-gap between the element and the glass. Just flick the switch and it de-mists and de-ices. Very efficiently. So efficiently that it's won nine safety and design awards. "SMITHS" rear window heaters come in 22½" and 30" sizes, as well as the twin 13" size for divided windows. Take a look through our rear window heaters soon.

50 Oxgate Lane, Cricklewood, London NW2 7JB.

REAR WINDOW HEATERS BY SMITHS INDUSTRIES
The people who show you how to be a better driver

PIRANHA
ELECTRONIC IGNITION

At last...a real advance in automotive ignition systems!

The PIRANHA system revolutionises normal car ignition systems. It has been designed to remove the inherent weakness of the mechanical contact breaker, whilst exploiting the proven advantages of the discharging inductive coil. Increased engine efficiency is achieved by producing a better, constant spark at all engine speeds, and this provides significant improvement in fuel consumption as well as a substantial reduction in exhaust pollution levels. Variants are available for a wide range of vehicles.

THE PIRANHA ADVANTAGES ARE-

MORE POWER

Nearly 40% more spark energy is produced than with a conventional contact breaker system, and this, combined with elimination of misfiring at all engine speeds, means more power for higher acceleration.

BETTER ECONOMY

The PIRANHA unit guarantees a better, more constant spark at all engine speeds, eliminating the high level of misfiring (potentially in excess of 4%) of the conventional contact breaker system at high revs. Completely burnt fuel therefore gives better fuel consumption.

LESS POLLUTION

Complete burning of fuel means that atmospheric pollution through the exhausting of unburnt fuel is substantially reduced.

EASIER STARTING

The PIRANHA unit produces full spark discharges independently of engine speed, even from a semi-discharged battery as low as 7 volts. The more powerful spark overcomes poor mixture, fouled plugs, and humidity problems, and guarantees faster, easier starting.

SIMPLICITY

Consisting of a small electronic switching unit (3¼" x 3" x ¼") and a light pulsing unit which fits into most existing distributors, the PIRANHA system can usually be fitted in less than ten minutes. Moving parts are kept to a minimum, and that means less wear and more dependability.

...AND THEY'VE BEEN PROVED!

Full testing at the University of Manchester Institute of Science and Technology has proved the PIRANHA Ignition to give an overall 37% increase in energy at the plugs in comparison with the conventional coil and contact breaker system.

37% EXTRA ENERGY

TRUST PIRANHA-
WE'VE PROVED IT WORKS

Price: **£19·80** inc. postage & packing, and V.A.T. "World Patents, subject to Crown User Agreement."

The Piranha Ignition is guaranteed for 12 months.

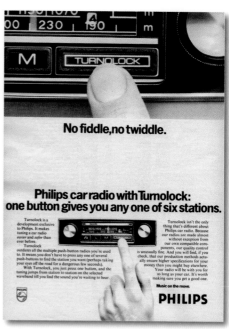
Aftermarket in-car entertainment systems were big business. Javelin offered both mono and stereo systems, with eight-track or cassette players, and the Phillips Turnolock removed the need to turn a knob to find the next radio station. One press on a button did the job.

were in favour. Whatever the colour, a vinyl roof – usually in black, or sometimes beige – seemed to set it off to perfection. Inside, the plastic upholstery in cheaper models had its own charms, such as stickiness and burning the backs of passengers' legs after the car had been left parked in the sun. The plusher interiors tended to be upholstered in furry fabrics – velours on the most expensive models – with their own distinctive smells. The layout of the instruments was usually functional and minimalist, mainly to reduce costs, while dashboards rattled and creaked, and there were often exposed wires underneath.

Beyond the new-car showroom, other factors affected the family motorist of the 1970s. From 1 January 1973, all new cars had to have reflective number plates, and many buyers fitted them to existing models to make them look newer. Safety belts were a big issue; it had been compulsory to fit them to front seats from 1967, but successive governments failed to make it compulsory to wear them during the 1970s.

The premature rusting of cars from the 1950s and 1960s made rustproofing a concern, and companies sprang up to underseal older cars. This meant spraying the underside with a rubber and bitumen compound that protected the metal underneath. It was sensible, but it would be a long time before car makers themselves made it standard on new cars. Under the bonnet, maintenance-free electronic ignition became available to replace the points that forever needed re-setting, and many family buyers settled for aftermarket conversions to make their lives easier. Stick-on rear window demister elements sold strongly because heated rear windows were far from universally available yet. Meanwhile, inside the cars, stereo radios gradually became more popular, and owners butchered door panels and parcels shelves to find somewhere to put the extra speakers. The tape cassette, too, quickly took over from the continuous-loop eight-track tape of the 1960s because it could be recorded at home; eight-track tapes were available only in pre-recorded form.

Tyres were more reliable than they had ever been, but punctures were still fairly common. Dunlop developed the 'run-flat' tyre in the 1970s, which re-inflated itself with foam after a puncture and could be used at low speed for a limited number of miles before being changed. Cost and a tendency for the tyres themselves to wear quickly killed this innovation. Tyre safety bands, which prevented a tyre from coming off the wheel rim after a catastrophic deflation, were another well-intentioned failure; their problem was cost and complication. And last but not least, it was during the 1970s that British police forces first began to use radar speed detectors. Cars – even family cars – were going faster.

The Dunlop Denovo run-flat tyre was one attempt to reduce the problems associated with punctures, but did not last.

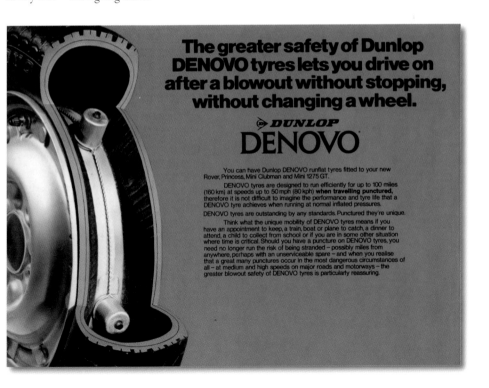

The greater safety of Dunlop DENOVO tyres lets you drive on after a blowout without stopping, without changing a wheel.

DUNLOP

DENOVO

You can have Dunlop DENOVO runflat tyres fitted to your new Rover, Princess, Mini Clubman and Mini 1275 GT.

DENOVO tyres are designed to run efficiently for up to 100 miles (160 km) at speeds up to 50 mph (80 kph) when travelling punctured, therefore it is not difficult to imagine the performance and tyre life that a DENOVO tyre achieves when running at normal inflated pressures.

DENOVO tyres are outstanding by any standards. Punctured they're unique.

Think what the unique mobility of DENOVO tyres means if you have an appointment to keep, a train, boat or plane to catch, a dinner to attend, a child to collect from school or if you are in some other situation where time is critical. Should you have a puncture on DENOVO tyres, you need no longer run the risk of being stranded – possibly miles from anywhere, perhaps with an unserviceable spare – and when you realise that a great many punctures occur in the most dangerous circumstances of all – at medium and high speeds on major roads and motorways – the greater blowout safety of DENOVO tyres is particularly reassuring.

It's here! The Vauxhall Chevette

It's a sporty coupé.

If you think the Chevette looks sporty and rakish just wait till you drive it. The gutsy 1256cc engine thrusts you from 0-60 in 15.3 seconds,* 50-70 in 14.6 seconds,* cruises the car effortlessly at 70, and gives a top speed of over 85 mph.* At any speed you'll appreciate the Chevette's remarkably light yet positive rack and pinion steering. Its superb road-holding and handling. Its braking power. (You've got a dual circuit, servo-assisted system, with discs at the front and self-adjusting drums at the rear.) And its economy. *In the 1975 Total Economy Run the Chevette recorded 45.3 mpg!*

It's a family saloon.

Thanks to its space-saving design the Chevette takes four adults in comfort with room to spare. (And we haven't forgotten the luggage.) But Chevette comfort means more than just space. It means reclining front seats, front seat belts, heated rear window, two-speed wipers plus intermittent wipe, electric screenwash, loop pile carpeting, complete underbody seal, radial tyres and reversing lights. Plus anti-burst door locks, energy absorbing body, facia and steering column. And all this is standard. If that isn't enough the Chevette 'L' gives you even more. Features like cloth trim, a clock, a cigarette lighter, opening rear quarter lights, a carpeted load deck and distinctive 'L' exterior trim.

It's a handy estate.

What do you do when you want to ca[rry] more bags and baggage than you can [get] into an ordinary car? Simply lift up the Chevette tailgate, fold down the back s[eat] and you'll be looking at 35.3 cubic fee[t] cargo space. Even with the rear seat i[n] there's 12.0 cubic feet† that takes lots [of] luggage. Or a small St. Bernard. So whether you want to carry people [in] comfort, or luggage in style, you can c[ount] on the Chevette. See it at your Vauxhall dealer now. It re[ally] the one car that's whatever you want it [to be.]

*Performance figures from Vauxhall's own p[erformance] tests. †AMA Cargo Volume Index.

There are two models available: the Chevette and the Chevette 'L'. All photographs shown are of the Chevette 'L'. Specifications correct at time of going to press.

CHEVETTE
It's whatever you want it to be.
Vauxhall

VAUXHALL GM

THE MARKET LEADERS: FORD AND VAUXHALL

THROUGHOUT THE 1970s, the two major manufacturers in the British family saloon market were Ford and Vauxhall. They were so much a part of the everyday scene that most buyers firmly believed them to be British, but both were American-owned, even though the cars were mostly built in Britain. Ford was an American company that had opened a factory in Britain in 1912, while Vauxhall had been a British company but had sold out to General Motors in 1925. Most important, perhaps, was that these two market leaders set the standard in dividing the market into four main segments. These segments were for entry-level models (mainly small hatchbacks, inspired by European designs), lower-medium saloons, upper-medium saloons, and large cars.

Both companies had been the key producers in the British family saloon market in the 1960s, too, but the major difference in the 1970s was that their British operations worked increasingly closely with their continental European equivalents – Ford's in Cologne, and Vauxhall's sister company, Opel, in Rüsselsheim. That the centre of each company's operations should have gravitated towards Germany was inevitable for two main reasons. The first was the acknowledged excellence of German engineering and manufacturing; the second was the increasing tendency of the British trade unions to disrupt car production through strike action.

Ford was an important name for family-car buyers. It may have stood to a degree for 'cheap and cheerful', but it also stood for affordable running costs, ubiquitous servicing expertise, and ready availability of parts. Parts for foreign cars were generally even more expensive in Britain than their British equivalents. Ford was the largest producer, and the cars it built were household names in Britain.

Ford's four-tier range started with the little Fiesta hatchback, which reached the market in 1976. Next up came the Escort, a small and fairly conventional family saloon. Above that came the best-selling Cortina, which offered more room and more performance. At the top of the range were the Consul and the Granada, two names for variants on a common design.

Opposite: From the start, Vauxhall emphasised the Chevette's versatility. While only the hatchback was on sale in June 1975, it could be a sporty coupé, a family saloon, or a handy estate (they said). A year later, there were booted saloons as well.

The Ford Cortina was the best-selling car of all in the 1970s. This publicity picture from the end of the decade celebrates four generations of the car: only the last two, here in blue and yellow, belonged to the 1970s.

None of these 1970s Fords had been wholly engineered in Britain, although examples of all were built at the company's Dagenham plant in Essex.

The Fiesta had been designed for pan-European production, and some cars sold in Britain had been built at Valencia in Spain, or at Saarlouis or Cologne in Germany. Even though a Ford with an engine driving the front wheels was a novelty in Britain, buyers were reassured that everything would be all right with the Fiesta simply because it was a Ford. There was nothing exceptional about it to worry them, either. It was easy to drive, it had adequate room for four passengers, and it consumed petrol at a refreshingly reasonable rate. It undoubtedly felt less sturdy than a Volkswagen Golf and handled with less aplomb than an Alfasud, but if it went wrong they could get it fixed easily and cheaply because Ford parts and servicing expertise were ubiquitous. That was what mattered. The car was a huge success, and Ford sold a million Fiestas between 1976 and the start of 1979.

Ford's Escort defined the lower-medium class, and its Mk1 model of 1968–74 was another million-seller. It was a three-box saloon with two or four doors, and there were practical but not especially roomy estate-car derivatives. Reliable, affordable, reasonably good-looking, and bathed in glamour from a factory-backed competitions programme, the Escort was replaced by a Mk2 version in 1974, which saw out the decade. Basically a re-skinned Mk1, this was squarer and sharper and, with a bigger 1.6-litre engine option as well, hinted that the whole range had moved upmarket.

The real success story belonged to the Cortina, however, which was Britain's best-selling car every year from 1972 to 1981. It defined the medium family saloon in Britain in the 1970s, not only by its physical

The Fiesta broke new ground for Ford, with its front-wheel-drive layout. This is a top-of-the-range Ghia version, with metallic paint, alloy wheels, a side bump strip and a sunroof among its desirable extras.

The Escort was a smart little family saloon, available with the usual Ford variety of trim levels and engines. This one is a MkI 1300GT four-door model, with the more powerful version of the 1.3-litre engine.

characteristics but also by the extent of its range. The Cortina beckoned the buyers of small saloons with an entry-level 1.3-litre engine, and offered a range of models right up to 2 litres, where it challenged the large saloons exemplified by Ford's own Consul.

The Cortina's secret was that it looked like a big car and, with the top equipment levels and bigger engines, it could make its owner feel as if he or she had gone up in the world. It made a roomy family car, and estate derivatives added practicality without compromising looks or noise levels. Handling was a little imprecise, but not out of step with the times, and the smallest 1.3-litre engines did struggle a little. So it was the 1.6-litre and 2.0-litre cars that defined the type.

The Cortina was also remarkably conservative. The model introduced in 1970 was a MkIII (the MkI having appeared in 1963) and was distinguished by an upward kick in its waistline, which reminded many of a Coca-Cola bottle's shape. Six years later, the 1976 MkIV Cortina needed little more than a visual makeover, with larger windows and straighter lines, and from 1979 the MkV brought only minor cosmetic differences.

Throughout this period, Ford gradually updated the mechanical elements, but buyers were generally far more interested in the equipment levels, which on the MkIII ran from base (unbadged) through L, XL and GT to GXL, with fake wood on doors and dash, plus spoke-styled wheels. On MkIV and later models, the designations changed a little, but the principle remained, and the Ghia badge, which indicated the luxury specification on one of these later Cortinas, would impress the neighbours.

The 1972 Granada set the benchmark for large saloons in the 1970s. Though the top-model Granadas were always too expensive for the family market, a smaller-engined Consul derivative (1970–5) was an affordable aspiration. Consuls were renamed Granadas too in 1975, but, when the facelifted Mk2 Granadas arrived in 1977, prices began to move out of family-saloon territory.

The MkII version of the Escort had the squarer lines that characterised 1970s cars, but underneath it was essentially the same car as the Mk1.

The dashboard of the Mk2 Escort was plain but quite stylish; the seats here have typical 1970s cloth facings combined with vinyl side panels.

The Granada family were Ford's big saloons in the 1970s. This is a MkI GXL model, too expensive for family buyers, but visually almost identical to the smaller-engined Consul, which was as far as most family budgets could stretch.

The Consuls and Granadas led the trend towards Europeanisation; these were not now British Fords but European Fords designed mainly in Germany. They were also vastly better cars than the models they replaced in almost every respect, and were available with the usual Ford range of trim levels. Most noticeable, though, was that they had five seats rather than the six of older large Fords: the gearchange was on the floor, and there were two individual front seats instead of a bench. Independent suspension all round gave them an unruffled ride, with good dynamics for such large cars.

Vauxhall came a strong second in the sales race. Like Ford, it arrayed its family cars in a four-tier range, but the individual models were deliberately positioned between the Fords rather than exactly matching them. The entry-level car was the Viva; next up was the newer Chevette; the Cavalier was the

The 1977 update of the Granada range brought the squarer styling lines associated with the 1970s. This is an entry-level Granada L – the car that took over from the old Consul as the family buyer's way into the Granada range.

The dash of the entry-level Mk2 Granada was quite stylish, although it featured many blank panels where more expensive variants had additional instruments and switches.

The Vauxhall Viva just crept into 1970 as an HB model but was replaced that year by the more sharply styled HC type, which saw out the decade.

Cortina rival, and the Victor and Ventora fought for sales with the Consul and Granada. Ventoras, though, shared bodyshells, but not engines or equipment, with the cheaper Victors, and were beyond the reach of most family buyers.

Directly competing with the cheaper Ford Escorts in the early 1970s was the Vauxhall Viva, the third generation of that name. Although bigger engines were available for enthusiasts, family buyers chose between 1,159cc and

The Chevette was Vauxhall's first hatchback, although the car was more expensive than the similarly sized Viva.

There was even more versatility for the Chevette · when two-door and four-door saloons were introduced alongside the hatchbacks.

1,256cc models, with fuel economy of around 30 mpg. Viva handling was disappointingly vague, but the model sold very well as a two-door, a four-door, or an estate, and lasted until 1980.

The Chevette started out as a brave attempt to match the small European hatchbacks that were attracting a big market share. Despite the Vauxhall griffin badge on the nose, it shared much of its engineering with cars built by General Motors subsidiaries in several other countries; and, with different trim and equipment levels, it was also sold in Britain as an Opel Kadett. This component sharing had ensured the Chevette stuck to old-style rear-wheel drive and a longitudinally mounted engine. This made it feel more like older designs to drive, and for some buyers there was much merit in that.

The Chevette became Britain's best-selling hatchback between 1975 and 1978, when it ceded that title to the Ford Fiesta. But it was also sold as an attractive booted four-door saloon and a three-door estate, both rather better suited to family use than the hatchback model. This versatility was a key selling

21

Above: The Victor
FD model had
been first with the
'Coca-Cola bottle'
styling in the
1960s, but lasted
only until 1972.

Centre and right:
The FE model
Victor brought
the straighter lines
associated with
the 1970s, but
somehow lacked
the character
of the older
FD model.
Its flat-faced
dashboard, too,
was uninspiring,
despite the fake
wood trim seen
in this example.

point, and Vauxhall's annoying television jingle ('It's whatever you want it to be! – A sporty coupé, a family saloon, a handy estate...') summed up its appeal rather well.

For the first half of the decade, Vauxhall's Cortina competitor was the Victor. The Coca-Cola bottle styling of the FD model (1967–72) had anticipated Ford by four years, but appearance was not everything: the Victor had a restricted choice of engines and trim levels, plus a reputation for poor build quality and premature rusting. Its ride felt oddly floaty, and so, unfortunately, did the steering. For the FE-type Victor (1972–8), Vauxhall borrowed underpinnings from the Opel Rekord and designed its own body. Much better built, more reassuring to drive, and faster as well, this was aimed at the top end of the Cortina market, with either 1.8-litre or 2.3-litre engines.

Meanwhile, the new Cavalier tackled the bottom end of the Cortina market from 1975. It had a conventional rear-wheel-drive layout, and a lot in common with the contemporary Opel Manta. Engines ranged from 1.3 litres right up to 2 litres, and two-door alternatives to the mainstream four-doors widened the range's appeal. Though the car looked smaller than a Cortina, it was a very able competitor on space and handling. With the Cavalier, Vauxhall rediscovered the formula for success and has never looked back.

Vauxhall's Cavalier sold very strongly and was a real alternative to Ford's Cortina.

BUILT IN BRITAIN: BRITISH LEYLAND AND CHRYSLER

T HE BRITISH CAR BUYER'S perception of the 1970s was coloured by the crisis that engulfed the British Leyland and Chrysler groups, and by the industrial action that very nearly sank both companies for good. These two groups encompassed all the major British car makers, and as such were widely seen as embodying the British car industry.

British Leyland had been formed at the government's insistence in 1968, to give the British motor industry a company big enough to compete with larger European makers such as Volkswagen and Renault. It remained British-owned throughout the period, while Chrysler's ownership was always foreign. Chrysler Europe was established in 1970, when its American Chrysler Corporation parent merged the French Simca company with the old Rootes Group companies it had bought in 1967 – Hillman, Humber, Singer and Sunbeam. It lasted until 1978, when Chrysler sold it to Peugeot, which renamed the company Talbot. This meant that some models had been Hillmans, Chryslers and Talbots within the space of less than ten years – which did nothing for customer confidence in the stability of the marque.

On its formation, the whole British Leyland operation had been put under the control of Leyland Motors, the hugely successful bus and truck manufacturer that already owned car makers Triumph and (since 1967) Rover. Amalgamation with the British Motor Corporation, which owned Austin, Morris, and several other names that were soon discarded, made the British Leyland Motor Corporation, later known simply as British Leyland (BL).

British Leyland's problem was that co-ordinating formerly rival manufacturers and streamlining their operations was a massive undertaking that was fiercely opposed by vested interests. Many of the changes needed to bring about a unified company met trade union resistance, and by 1974 the company was on its knees. It turned to the government for help, and in 1975 British Leyland was nationalised. It spent the rest of the decade struggling with outdated products and insufficient capital to develop new ones.

By and large, Austin and Morris were the least expensive BL marques, while the smaller Triumphs were more expensive alternatives. Wolseleys were

Opposite:
The dashboard
of the Austin
Princess provided
comprehensive
instrumentation,
and the velour-
trimmed seats
were very
comfortable.

One thing that hardly changed on the Mini was its uncompromisingly spartan dashboard. This is a very early car, with cable-operated door releases.

The Mini was an evergreen favourite, and this is the Clubman variant. It sold well abroad, too, as this Swiss-market picture suggests.

better-equipped Austins or Morrises, but died out in 1975. Other BL models were not for family buyers: MG built sports cars, Triumph had both sports cars and more expensive sports saloons, while Rover, Jaguar and Daimler built luxury cars.

There was an estate version of the Morris Marina. This view shows the load space available when the rear seat was folded down – and the uninspiring moulded plastic trim.

The Marina was a deliberately simple design, intended to challenge the Cortina. These two date from the end of the 1970s, when the original 1.8-litre engine had been replaced by a newer 1.7-litre in the 1700 model.

Even so, British Leyland had some models of character, and its sales benefited from patriotic allegiance. The entry-level family car was the Mini, a trend-setter in its time, but eleven years old by 1970. Though uncomfortable for tall drivers and cramped for families with teenage

27

children, it was still enormously popular and much loved, not least for its cheeky appearance, and the small size that made it easy to park and cheap to run. Above the Mini in size, the BL range offered three choices. Cheapest was the Morris Marina, next the Austin Allegro, and most expensive the Triumph Dolomite.

The Marina was deliberately conventional, and ineffectively challenged the Ford Cortina range. It came as a four-door saloon, a reasonably capacious estate or, bizarrely, a two-door coupé that was irrelevant in the family-saloon market. Marinas were dull cars, and pedestrian to drive. Though they offered adequate passenger space, passengers sat on either unyielding vinyl or a strange-smelling nylon cloth upholstery. Yet Marinas found willing buyers among those who wanted a simple, basic family car.

Allegros were certainly distinctive, but dumpy rather than attractive. Their appeal lay in more sophisticated and modern engineering than was available on the similarly priced Marina.

At first glance, the Allegro seemed to be a direct competitor for the Marina, but it was a deliberately more adventurous design aimed at different customers. It had front-wheel drive rather than the Marina's rear-wheel drive; it had much sharper (though far from pretty) styling; and its whole character was forward-looking rather than conventional. A memorable characteristic was the 'quartic' steering wheel on early cars, with flattened sides to give more thigh room for the driver. Unfortunately, it did suffer

from quality-control problems, and its nickname of 'All-aggro' ('aggro' being contemporary slang for 'aggravation') reflected its reputation and patchy build quality. That the Allegro sold less well than the Marina confirmed BL's assumption that most family buyers did not want sophistication.

The small Triumphs supposedly had more breeding. The 1500 (1970–3) had front-wheel drive, but this was abandoned when the company wanted to fit more powerful engines. Re-engineered with rear-wheel drive, the car was renamed the Toledo (1970–6), and then the Dolomite (1976–80). With the smallest engine options, it had none of the sporting promise of the Triumph name, but the Dolomite 1850 (1976–80) was capable of 100 mph, and the

Estate-car derivatives of family saloons were popular, too. This was the Allegro derivative – not very capacious, but quirky enough to look at and big enough for the family dog.

Triumph's Dolomite did not lack style, although its basic engineering was conservative. This is the 1.5-litre 1500 model.

29

With vinyl roof, smart wheels and a side stripe, this was the aspirational high-performance Sprint model Dolomite.

Opposite, top: The Maxi – strictly an Austin, but latterly rarely called that – was an enormously practical design, and spacious too. Unfortunately, good looks were not part of the deal.

Sprint (1973–80) could reach 115 mph. With nicely appointed interiors that featured wood trim, Toledos and Dolomites were certainly a cut above Marinas and Allegros, but were pricier too.

The Austin Maxi (1969–81) had the unenviable task of challenging the Ford Cortina for sales, while the Marina and Allegro snapped at its heels. Its strange looks came about because it shared an admittedly large cabin with the bigger 1800 and 2200 models. It was advanced, too, combining front-wheel drive and the hatchback configuration otherwise found only on the Renault 16 in this market sector. Early examples had a memorably awful cable-operated gearchange, and the spare wheel exposed under the rear ensured that wheel-changing was always a messy operation. Quality-control problems held it back too, and it suffered in the 1970s from the general public mistrust of anything associated with British Leyland.

Those 1800 and 2200 models came as Austins, Morrises, or as upmarket Wolseleys with better trim and equipment levels. The model designations initially belonged to the mould-breaking 'Land Crab' types (1964–75), so called because of their somewhat ungainly appearance. Yet these were good cars, providing a roomy interior in a relatively compact size because of a space-efficient front-wheel-drive layout. They were dependable and durable large saloons.

From 1975, they were replaced by similarly space-efficient '18–22 series' saloons with the same manufacturers' names. These were admirable family cars, although their advanced Hydragas suspension had no means of compensating for a boot full of heavy luggage, and power-assisted steering

was an essential extra-cost option. Unfortunately, their new wedge-shaped styling was too much for many buyers, while the uncertainty brought about by the government's rescue of British Leyland and a sudden name change to 'Princess' in 1976 both took their toll. BL had missed a trick, too, by not making them hatchbacks.

Chrysler entered the 1970s with two older models. Its small car was the Imp, and the Hillman Hunter its family saloon. More expensive was the Humber Sceptre, a Hunter derivative with the wood and leather traditionally associated with the Humber marque, and carefully priced at the top of the family saloon market.

The basic Hillman Imp (1963–76) was accompanied by a Sunbeam Sport version (1966–76) with a little more power and performance. Other derivatives had been dropped at the end of the 1960s because of declining sales. The Imp featured unconventional technology to make room for four people within its compact body: engine and transmission were both at the rear, and that worried more traditionally minded buyers. That the engine proved troublesome and the car rusted quickly were serious deterrents to anyone hesitating between an Imp and the Mini, from which it had been intended to steal sales. So although Imps handled well and offered the kind of fuel economy that

Below: Despite the wood veneer trim, there was still something desperately unadventurous about the Maxi's dashboard. Yet it offered enough for family buyers.

The Princess – originally known as the 18–22 series – had a strikingly modern wedge-shaped design and appealed to better-off families. This 2000HLS model dates from the later 1970s, when a vinyl roof was still a desirable feature.

The Hillman Imp was an advanced design when new in the 1960s, but by the 1970s its shortcomings were well known and production lasted only until 1976.

buyers wanted in the 1970s, the word was already out that buying one was a risky proposition. As a result, the Imp was dropped before it had a chance to carry Chrysler badges.

By contrast, the Hunter embodied deliberately conventional engineering. It was a staid and unexceptional three-box saloon with a body style that was perhaps too similar to the contemporary Ford Cortina MkII. One result was that it immediately looked old-fashioned when the MkIII Cortina arrived for 1971, although the car did linger on until 1979, after being re-badged as a Chrysler in 1977. The Humber Sceptre derivative disappeared in 1976.

Hillman's Avenger sold well, although it offered nothing very special in standard form. Most were four-door saloons or estates. The moulded vinyl upholstery is clearly visible on this two-door saloon.

However, Chrysler had high hopes of the new cars it introduced in 1970: the Hillman Avenger (1970–6) and the Chrysler 180 (1970–80) – the latter being the first European model to bear the new marque name. Competing with the Escort, Marina and Viva, the Avenger was a thoroughly conventional three-box saloon with rear-wheel drive, although an imaginative treatment of the rear-window pillar gave it a distinctive visual character. Saloons had four doors or, from 1973, two. There were estate derivatives as well, plus sporty GT and better-trimmed GLS versions. Later models bore Chrysler (from 1977) and Talbot (from 1979) badges. Avengers arrived just in time for the vinyl-roof craze, and looked all the better with one, especially when strong colour contrasts were used.

The Avenger had been drawn up under the old regime and, in a curious echo of BL's Marina/Allegro thinking, the merger with Simca resulted in a

The Chrysler Alpine was a French design, and much more modern in approach than the saloons from the British side of Chrysler Europe.

second model positioned just above it. The Chrysler Alpine (1975–9, and later as a Talbot) was quite different from the Avenger, and a good car, too: essentially a French Simca design built in Britain for the British market, it had front-wheel drive and a hatchback, and won the Car of the Year award on its introduction. Perhaps not as sharply styled as it deserved to be, it was also too softly sprung and had rather ordinary handling.

Chrysler's 180 and its 2-litre derivative were initially too expensive to appeal to family buyers, but later price realignments brought them within reach. They offered more cabin room than the company's cheaper saloons, and were based on a design originally intended for a new Humber. However, the deliberate visual resemblance to the Avenger probably cheapened them in buyers' eyes, and these cars simply lacked sparkle.

Towards the end of the decade, Chrysler reinvented its small-car range, basing the new hatchback Sunbeam (1977–9, and a Talbot thereafter) on a shortened Avenger platform. With rear-wheel drive, the Sunbeam was out of step with industry trends, and the rear end could hop noticeably on rough roads, but the car was conventional enough to appeal to traditional buyers who could live with its three-door configuration. Perhaps more memorable than the car was the television advertisement, in which family-favourite singer Petula Clark encouraged viewers to 'put a little Sunbeam in your life'.

In the 1970s it was always important to have attractive girls to draw photographers to a Motor Show stand, as Chrysler did when launching the 180 saloon.

Changes of identity did nothing to boost customer confidence in cars such as the Sunbeam, which started out as a Chrysler and then became a Talbot. It marked the start of yet another new approach for Chrysler.

After the Sunbeam came a five-door hatchback based on a shortened Alpine platform. The Horizon (1978–9, and then a Talbot) was Chrysler's first attempt at a 'world car', and was sold as a Simca in France, although Dodge and Plymouth versions in the United States had many differences. Strangely characterless inside, the Horizon nevertheless had proper legroom in the rear and gave a comfortable ride. It handled well, though failings were heavy steering and a woolly gearchange, plus an engine that became loud when used hard. Styling then seen as crisp helped the Horizon to win European Car of the Year in 1979, but its appearance dated quite quickly.

Customers who wanted a small car with five doors had to wait for the Chrysler Horizon, which became a Talbot Horizon after just one year on sale.

FRENCH AND ITALIAN FLAIR

CITROËN, PEUGEOT, RENAULT AND SIMCA were the French makers whose cars had a major impact on the family-saloon market in 1970s Britain. None of them was a newcomer: all had been gradually building market share over the last decade or more and were able to take advantage of the British makers' difficulties between 1970 and 1980. The French excelled at making family-friendly cars, but heavy taxation on larger engines in France encouraged them to focus on space-efficient designs with small-capacity engines.

Citroën was still selling the 2CV model, originally designed as an economy car and in production since 1948. It was slow, noisy, and offered little in the way of crash protection, but many families with very young children bought the 2CV because it was cheap to buy and cheap to run. Despite very soft suspension that allowed alarming body-roll on corners, the car handled safely and could be hustled along rapidly up to around 60 mph. More sophisticated derivatives, the Dyane and the Ami, offered the same blend of qualities with more modern body styling – but they were always seen as quirky.

That quirkiness also characterised Citroën's larger GS, new in 1970. Owners soon got used to the odd exhaust note from its flat-four engines, to the superb ride that depended on a high-pressure hydro-pneumatic system that was not easy for the owner himself to work on, and to the excellent all-disc brakes. Only the uninspiring interiors let these cars down, with drab upholstery in typical French family-car style contrasting markedly with the almost futuristic instrument display and single-spoke steering wheel. Above the GS, the big Citroëns were much admired but were priced beyond the means of most families.

Citroën was wholly owned by Peugeot after 1976, but there was little cross-fertilisation between the two marques at this stage. Peugeot remained defiantly conventional – by French standards, at least. Its 104 'supermini' of 1972 managed to make even the latest hatchback style seem dull, although the car was notable for being a family-friendly four-door model when other

Opposite:
Though the interior trim was quite basic, there was plenty of room in a Renault 12, and the seats were surprisingly comfortable.

The Dyane was a more sophisticated variation of the 2CV – but still cheap, as this 1976 advertisement attempted to persuade the public.

The Citroën 2CV was an elderly design that offered basic motoring for families at minimal cost.

The £1420 hatchback.

● 5 doors
● Sunshine roof
● Jersey cloth upholstery
● Up to 51mpg ('Autocar' Economy Car Test 15.3.75)
● Cheap to maintain and insure
● Amazingly high resale value

Test drive a Dyane, or write for brochure and dealer list.
Citroën Cars Ltd, Dept D10, Mill Street, Slough SL2 5DE.

Stylish, 5-door, 51mpg Citroën Dyane

CITROËN ♦ DYANE

cars in its class had just two doors. Those extra doors brought extra size and weight, and the 104 always felt underpowered, so owners had to get used to frequent gearchanging if they were to keep up with other traffic. The steering was rather woolly, too, and the vinyl seats could become sticky when hot.

The 304 (1969–80) was the mid-sized Peugeot, though expensive enough to need the space efficiency that came with its transverse engine and front-wheel drive. These modern features did not lift it out of the ordinary because it was really a repackaged version of the older 204, but it was solid and durable, though rather stodgy to drive. The big 504 was too expensive to attract family buyers in the early 1970s, but Peugeot kept its price down and by the end of the decade it was a contender.

The GS saloons had the same remarkable self-levelling hydraulic suspension as the bigger Citroëns, and embodied a curious mix of advanced engineering and French quirkiness. This is a top-model GS 1220, with 1.2-litre engine and the top Pallas trim and equipment level.

Peugeot's 104 was more than just another small hatchback, with its family-friendly four-door configuration, but it was no thing of beauty.

The Peugeot 104's dashboard was fairly typical of the times. Note the sporty red stripes on the seats of this later model, designed to create a 'hot hatch' ambience.

Good-looking, owing to Peugeot's long-term association with Italian design house Pininfarina, it had standard-setting diesel engines as well. The 504 had conventional rear-wheel drive, but with roomy passenger cabins and viceless handling. Estate derivatives had huge carrying capacity or seven forward-facing seats, and fuel-injected top models were quick, too.

Clever styling and front-wheel drive made the Peugeot 304 seem less ordinary than it really was, and reliability counted in its favour.

The cheapest Renault was the 4, an elderly design that was square and ugly, but its low cost and spaciousness ensured its survival right through the 1970s. Over-soft suspension was typically French; so was the odd 'pull-and-twist gearchange protruding from the dash; and the Renault 4 was not speedy. Yet with four doors it was good basic family transport.

More exciting was the Renault 5, new in 1972 and evidence that the French engineers had been thinking along the same lines as those at Fiat who had come up with the 127 a year earlier. Above all, though, the car had

Middle and right: The 504 was Peugeot's large saloon, but its cost was a stretch for family buyers. If a capacious estate was needed, though, the Peugeot did the job better than most.

a unique look, which was achieved mainly by its grey plastic bumpers that blended into the lines of the body. Most other cars still had chromed metal bumpers that stuck out in front and behind. The plastic bumpers tended to discolour after a few years, but they did absorb all manner of parking knocks that would have left traditional bumpers misshapen, and they did not rust.

Though small, the 5 had good cabin room in the French tradition. It had some endearing features, too. Among them was the position of the spare wheel, mounted over the nose of the engine under the bonnet. It tended to get dirty very quickly, and that was a major deterrent to checking oil and water levels on the engine. There was a lump under the dashboard where the engine protruded into the passenger cabin, and owners of early cars also had to get accustomed to a pull-and-twist gear lever like that of the Renault 4. When Renault realised that the car was an international success, they changed that for a more conventional floor-mounted gearshift in 1973.

Renault's mid-range family saloon was the 12 (1969–80), a surprisingly conventional three-box design with front-wheel drive and an estate alternative. It offered good passenger accommodation, and its curvaceous style helped it to stand out from other lower-medium saloons, but the engines were noisy and the steering disappointingly heavy. Neither factor stopped it from appealing very strongly to the family market, where its comfort was a strong selling point.

Further up the family-saloon range, Renault settled for being different with the 16 (1965–79), which was the inspiration behind the British Maxi. Some interior features of this hatchback were strange, and the column-mounted gearchange was at odds with contemporary practice, though much

The Renault 4 was another old design, but it was practical enough to retain family appeal right through the 1970s and beyond.

Renault's 12
was surprisingly
orthodox for a
French family
saloon, and proved
a big hit in Britain.

more user-friendly than the push-pull type in the smaller Renaults. Yet this
was a ground-breaking and much-liked car that combined the best features
of both saloon and estate designs. Like many Renaults, though, it had to be
taken to a Renault dealer for repair work, as special tools were required for
some jobs. The 20, which began to replace it from 1975, was larger and more
expensive, so the 16 remained in the catalogues to keep family buyers happy.

The Simca marque disappeared from Britain in the mid-1970s, when its
new products were badged as Chryslers, but at the start of the decade
a favourite was the four-door 1100 model. With the engine mounted
transversely and driving the front wheels, the cabin was left free of
transmission-tunnel intrusions. It went and stopped well, too, but its looks
were an acquired taste. Yet it was affordable, gave a comfortable if rather firm
ride, and had all the family practicality for which French cars were famous.
Its disadvantage was early and severe rusting.

Opposite:
The Renault 16
was a pioneering
design that
brought hatchback
versatility to the
mid-sized family
saloon in the mid-
1960s and sold
strongly in Britain
during the early
1970s. The boot
was large and
became larger still
when the rear seat
was folded away
and the parcels
shelf removed.

As in France, the national characteristics of Italian cars in the 1970s were
dictated by the domestic taxation system. Big engines incurred big taxes, and
so the Italian makers generally kept their engines smaller than 2 litres and
extracted maximum performance from them. In Britain, Italian cars were
perceived as sporty, with high-revving engines. They were also thought
of as tinny and chronically rust-prone, and generally with good reason.
Alfa Romeo, Fiat and Lancia all suffered from the same faults, and their larger
saloons were never an everyday sight on British roads.

But the models that changed the way British buyers thought about small
family cars in the 1970s both came from Italy. At the time, that seemed a
most unlikely quarter, but punitive tax regulations on big engines had forced

Italian designers to think small for many years, and so the Alfasud from Alfa Romeo and the 127 from Fiat were logical developments.

Both were announced in 1971, and both went on sale in Britain a year or so later. Both were small-engined cars that were intended to be cheap to run, and both had fairly cramped back seats; the children, who were most likely to travel in the back, had to clamber in past tilted front seats on the two-door Fiat. Oddly, both cars shared a similar overall outline, too, with a sloping rear window and no separate, protruding boot. But there was much more room in these little Italian saloons than most people realised, not least because their engines drove the front wheels, so there was no transmission tunnel to take up space inside the passenger cabin.

Their characters, though, were very different. Alfa Romeo was known for its sporting characteristics, which were as evident

in its saloons as in its sports cars. Based in Milan, the company had been persuaded by the Italian government to build a new factory in southern Italy (hence the Alfasud name, which translated as 'Alfa South') to alleviate unemployment there. What was needed was a car that would sell in big numbers, and the choice fell on this new small family model. Small family car it may have been, but it was still very much an Alfa Romeo. Its engine had a

Above: When the Fiat 127 took on a hatchback, it created a whole new sub-genre of small car, which later became known as the 'supermini' class.

Once a car has proved its economy, reliability, practicality, performance and comfort, what's left?

There is more in the making of a great car than those five important elements. There's the continuous striving for improvement which plays a big part in the production of each Simca.

The new 1976 Simcas are made to last. The 1100 models have a refined gearbox for easy handling. As for the 1000 models, increased sound insulation gives you an even quieter ride. There's also improved low speed torque.

And just as Chrysler feels it's important to improve their cars, they also feel it's important to bring out new models. Such as the 1100 LX.

Here's a car that gives you up to 38 mpg! It's very generous when it comes to other things, too. Front disc brakes, front

wheel drive, and front seat belts. But what makes the LX special is the side styling treatment (bold stripes along either side), the sporty road wheels, the black finish grille, plush cloth trim, head restraints, soft rim steering wheel, dipping mirror, reversing lights and a very handy opening rear door that leads to a big loading space.

Another new car is the 1000 SR. The grille and windscreen wipers are black finished, the wheels are ventilated, the mirror dips (if you want it to) and the upholstery is trimmed with check cloth. The 1000 SR gives up to 36 mpg† and also has front disc brakes, and front seat belts.

Prove it yourself with a test drive at your Chrysler dealer.

1100 LX.

Simca '76
More than ever.

SIMCA

CHRYSLER
UNITED KINGDOM

†Manufacturer's figures.

Few French family cars were conventionally attractive, and the Simca 1100 was no exception. The side stripes – actually decals – on this 1100LX model were a desirable option that did improve the car's appearance.

sporting bark, the gearchange was slick, and it could be hustled through a succession of bends with enthusiasm and under complete control. Not surprisingly, there was soon a demand for more powerful engines, and Alfa Romeo responded appropriately.

Fiat, on the other hand, had an altogether more mundane, middle-of-the-road image in Britain. It was known for its reliable but rather ordinary saloons, and British buyers would perhaps have described earlier Fiats as 'tinny'. There was undoubtedly a perceived flimsiness about the cars, and that carried

over to the new 127. It was in many ways just a variation on an earlier small Fiat, the much more orthodox 128, but what made the 127 stand out was its hatchback.

Hatchbacks were not new, but they were new to small family saloons. By the time the Fiat 127 arrived, the Renault 16 and the Austin Maxi had firmly established hatchback practicality among medium-sized family cars. In fact, the 127 originally had an ordinary fixed rear window and a little boot lid underneath. It was only after it had been on sale for a year that its makers redesigned its sloping rear window to lift up and give access to the boot. Better yet, they arranged for the rear seat back to fold forwards so that the boot space could be extended all the way to the backs of the front seats. For a small car, the little Fiat had extraordinary load-carrying capacity and a degree of versatility that others in its class lacked. These qualities persuaded many buyers to forgive its starkly simple interior, poor gearchange and noisy engine.

Fiat also produced some middle-sized saloons. They entered the 1970s with the 124 (1966–74), which came as a well-proportioned, if rather square-looking, four-door saloon or estate. Though an elderly design, the 124 handled well owing to its front-wheel drive, and stopped well on all-round disc brakes. Rapid rusting did it no favours, but the basic design continued in production for many years after sale to the Russian Lada company. The replacement for the 124 was the 131 (1974–84), often called the Mirafiori after the factory in Turin where it was built. This again came in saloon and estate forms, and was competent enough as a Cortina competitor, but had still not overcome the rust problem.

Fiat's 124 had well-balanced lines, despite its boxy shape. Unfortunately, premature rusting made it a bold choice as a family saloon.

45

THE SENSIBLE CHOICES: GERMAN AND SWEDISH

THE 'SENSIBLE' CHOICES as family cars in Britain in the 1970s were those built in Germany and Sweden. Both countries produced cars that were solid, well engineered and durable – although buyers often had to pay a premium to obtain these qualities. That they were qualities which appealed to family motorists explains their success.

The German marques that mattered to the average buyer in the 1970s were Opel and Volkswagen; BMW and Mercedes were far too expensive to secure family-saloon sales, and the only affordable Audi was the 80, which was right on the edge of the £1,500 break-point that unofficially defined family-car prices in the first half of the decade. It was never very popular. Because Mercedes and BMW prices were high, buyers tended to think that all German cars were expensive, although Volkswagen's Beetle certainly was not. German cars were nevertheless seen as well-engineered and reliable, with good standards of safety, even if they were sometimes lacking in excitement.

As already explained, Opel belonged to General Motors, which also owned Vauxhall. As Europeanisation gathered pace in the car industry, the two marques ended up producing the same cars with different badges, but for the first half of the 1970s there were also distinctive Opels.

The entry-level Opel was the Kadett, which was a rather ordinary lower-medium saloon with an estate derivative. The original car (1965–73) gave way to a new model (1973–9) that was essentially the same as the Vauxhall Viva. Opel's best-seller in the United Kingdom for the first half of the 1970s, however, was the Ascona. This was a credible competitor to Ford's Cortina, and its solid build quality gave it an appeal beyond its conventional layout and pedestrian looks. Yet it was priced dangerously close to that £1,500 mark, and many buyers felt they could get better value for their money from elsewhere. As for the bigger Opels, the Rekord introduced in 1972 had much in common with the Vauxhall Victor, but was markedly more expensive, and beyond the reach of the typical family buyer.

Volkswagens were determinedly not expensive. The rear-engined Beetle was elderly and noisy, but a favourite with young families on the

Opposite:
The design of
Saab's 96 was
timeless – which
was just as well,
because it was old
by the 1970s. This
version of the car
had a Ford V4
engine.

This is a two-door
Kadett saloon
of the type
introduced in
1973; the styled
wheels were
typical of Opel,
although the side
stripe was not
standard on cars
for the British
market.

grounds of affordability, if little else. It remained in production until 1977
while its makers tried desperately to develop a replacement. Their first
efforts were the 1600 saloon and its Variant estate derivative, followed by
the 411 and 412. But all these were little more than re-bodied Beetles and
were too expensive for family buyers.

The Opel Ascona
was a solid and
reliable small
family saloon, again
related to Vauxhall
models, but with
distinctive Opel
touches.

Volkswagen made a more determined effort in the early 1970s,
announcing the new Passat (1973–80) in the lower-medium sector. This came
as a saloon, hatchback or estate, with sharp new Italian styling and front-end
panelling shared with the Audi 80. Its front engine and front-wheel drive
were in tune with customer expectations of the time, and the Passat had solid,
middle-class appeal. From 1979, it capitalised on its 'sensible' appeal with a

The Volkswagen Beetle was very basic in many respects, but buyers were impressed by its simplicity and its reliability.

frugal diesel-engine option. However, Volkswagen's greatest success was its entry into the small hatchback market, announced in 1974 as the Golf.

The Golf was right in line with current thinking, with a conventional water-cooled engine mounted transversely at the front and driving the front wheels. Like the Passat, it had distinctive angular styling that had originated in Italy. Beetles had built up a reputation for mechanical simplicity and reliability – which meant cheap motoring – and the Golf inherited that reputation and built on it. The quality of its construction was immediately apparent, too, and although the dashboard was essentially a large plastic box, it was rigidly made and did not creak like those on some of its rivals, and the instruments in it were clear and logically laid out.

The Audi 80 of the early 1970s was not a great success in Britain, but this small family saloon pointed the way forwards for the Volkswagen range.

Compare the front-end details of this Mk I Volkswagen Passat with those of the Audi 80. This stylish-looking family car was more stodgy than it looked, but good reliability ensured its success.

Above all, the Golf was easy to drive and had far more grip than a small-engined hatchback needed – and that characteristic made it an ideal candidate for a larger engine. Two years after its introduction, the companion Golf GTi model was introduced. It may not have been the first 'hot hatchback' – the slightly earlier Renault 5 Gordini (called Alpine in its native France) claimed that title – but it was the one that made the most impact.

While the Golf supplied the top end of the small-car market for Volkswagen, the company also had a smaller car for the lower end of that market. Things had not been planned in quite that way, and the smaller car had originated as an Audi 50 in 1974. A year later, largely as a result of the Golf's success, its specification was adjusted and it was also made available as the Volkswagen Polo. The Audi version disappeared a few years later; the Polo became a favourite entry-level small car in Britain.

The same front-end look is clear on this Volkswagen Golf, the small hatchback that quickly became the benchmark car of its type. This is a Golf Driver special edition for the British market, dating from 1979.

With 2½ inches less length between front and rear wheels, the Polo was inevitably less spacious than the Golf, and therefore less viable as a family car – but many young families struggled with its uniformly two-door configuration and strapped their babies into the back seat. It also had a less substantial feeling to it than the Golf, although the Polo was still a solid little car with many similarities to its bigger sibling. Bright colours – yellows, reds and greens were favourites – gave it a special appeal to younger owners, and running costs were even more affordable than those of the Golf.

The 1970s was a very successful period in Britain for the Swedish car makers Volvo and Saab. Volvo in particular was perceived as a sensible, safe and solid middle-class choice; excitement was foreign to the marque at that stage, but its buyers were unconcerned. Volvos seemed to be indestructible,

The Golf GTI went on to set new standards, combining hatchback practicality with strong performance and sporty handling. It still worked as family transport, too.

Blocky, chunky and plasticky – this was the dashboard of the Golf, in typical 1970s style. This is a GTI model.

The Polo was neat and practical, and maintained the new VW family 'face'.

either by accidents or by deterioration, and that was the important factor. Both Volvo and Saab had a successful rallying history.

Volvo's greatest success came with their big saloons, the 145 and later 245 models, although these were too expensive to interest the average family buyer. However, the company had also acquired two smaller designs with the purchase of the Dutch DAF company. These were the 66 (1975–80) and the 343 (1976–91).

The little two-door 66 was always too flimsy to be a proper Volvo, but it had its own appeal as a city runabout, together with plenty of character. Its engines were bought in from Renault, and drove through an unusual Continuously Variable Transmission (called Variomatic) that worked like a stepless automatic and made the cars feel slower than they really were. Practicality and simplicity were the 66's main attractions.

Surprisingly, perhaps, the dashboard of the Polo was neater and more user-friendly than that of the more expensive Golf. This is a 1975 car.

The three-door 343 had been more thoroughly re-engineered after Volvo took it on, but still had Renault engines and Variomatic gearboxes – at least until 1979, when a manual alternative arrived. It did have the solid feel of the bigger Volvos, and had the marque's traditional 'safe and sensible' appeal, but was singularly ordinary to drive, and played only a bit part in the family-saloon market because of its lack of rear doors. (These eventually arrived on the 345 in 1980.)

Saab was very different and was a much more adventurous choice for a family car. The company's aircraft-industry connections gave it a more forward-looking image, and the cars

The Volvo 66 had started life as a Dutch DAF. It never made a convincing Volvo but was a handy, if somewhat staid, city car for small families.

were very different from the ultra-conservative Volvos. They combined similar durability with greater driving fun and much more character.

Saab entered the decade with one old and one new model. The old one was the 96 saloon (the estate version was a 95), which combined a modern Ford engine with a shape introduced in 1960 but even older in inspiration. With just two doors, the car had its limits for family use, but its dynamic qualities were surprisingly good and the drive was let down only by a cumbersome gearchange mounted on the steering column. The newer 99, however, marked the beginning of a move upmarket for the company and was simply too expensive for family buyers.

The Volvo 343 was available only with three doors in the 1970s, but its family appeal was broadened when a five-door 345 variant appeared later. Though initial design was done by DAF, it was a real small Volvo by the time it went on sale.

EASTERN PROMISE: THE SOVIET BLOC AND JAPAN

L OW-COST MOTORING was as much a preoccupation for many people in the 1970s as it has been since, and the increasing cost of petrol in that decade increased the demand for cheap cars. The situation was tailor-made for importing low-cost cars from abroad, and cars made in the countries of the Soviet bloc were as cheap as they came – because of low labour costs where they were built. So Lada, Polski-Fiat, Skoda and Wartburg all found local importers and tried to make their mark.

Yet these Soviet bloc cars were never big sellers. Build quality was universally poor, designs were outdated, and there was still a social stigma attached to ownership of such vehicles at a time when the Cold War kept East and West at nuclear loggerheads. Depreciation was high, too, and the dealer networks were sparse. Low purchase price was their main appeal, as it was for many of the cars that came flooding out of Japan during the 1970s. The difference was that the Japanese cars were well built, and their designs gradually improved as time went on.

The Russian Lada and Polish Polski-Fiat were both based on old Italian Fiat designs. The Lada was really a Russian-built Fiat 124, a square-rigged four-door saloon from the 1960s that was both mechanically simple and determinedly rugged. That ruggedness affected the detail finish as well, and Ladas were quite crudely built, with little in the way of equipment. The original 1200 and 1300 models (1974–88 in Britain) were supplemented by 1500s and 1600s from 1977, but the cars gained nothing in appeal from their new and larger engines, which remained as noisy and unrefined as the earlier types.

The basis of the Polski-Fiat 125P, as its name suggested, was the Fiat 125. This in turn was more or less a longer edition of the 124 with more interior room, and also dated from the 1960s; real Fiat 125s had a newer engine, but the Polish models had the older 124 types. British imports began in 1975 and, like the Ladas, had low levels of equipment and refinement to go with their low showroom prices. From 1978, the 125P was joined by the Polonez, a slightly restyled hatchback derivative of the same design. It was still crude, though, and did not sell well.

The Polish-built Polski-Fiat 125P was simply an old Fiat design assembled in Poland – though its noisy engine was from a previous generation of Fiats.

Wartburgs were built in East Germany and were best known for the clouds of smelly exhaust produced by their three-cylinder, two-stroke engines – the last of their type available on a production car in Britain. Front-wheel drive did not redeem their handling, which was universally regarded as bad. The cars came as 'Knight' saloons and 'Tourist' estates, but their only virtue, apart from cheapness, was that they had spacious passenger cabins. Build quality was tinny, and the three-box styling was basic and totally without charm. Introduced in 1966, they lasted only until the middle of the 1970s in Britain, when they were outlawed on exhaust emissions grounds.

Far more common were Czechoslovakian-built Skodas. Skoda had been a major innovator before the Soviet era, but the design of their S100, bigger-engined S110 and later Estelle saloons was crude, and the

From East Germany came the Wartburg, seen here in Tourist estate guise.

55

The Czechoslovakian Skoda S100L was an evil-handling car with old-fashioned suspension and its engine at the rear. Low cost was its main appeal – as this 1973 advertisement shows, it cost only £796.

construction perhaps cruder. Their cabins always smelled of low-grade plastic and rubber, their controls were unrefined, and their ride was sometimes turbulent. With noisy rear-mounted engines putting the weight where the old-fashioned swing-axle rear suspension could cope least with it, they were easy to 'lose' in hard cornering and were twitchy in strong cross-winds. The Estelle of 1977 was better styled than the earlier saloons (1970–80), but was still no looker. Interior space and low showroom prices remained its only virtues.

There was a fastback coupé version of the Skoda, though with less family appeal. This was the 110R model.

The Skoda Estelle was a makeover of older models, with most of the same inherent problems, but it was cheap.

By contrast with the relative failure of the Soviet bloc imports, one of the most striking phenomena in the automotive world in Britain during the 1970s was the success of Japanese cars. It was almost wholly unexpected; the few Japanese cars that had been imported in the 1960s had been strange, crude models with engineering based firmly on 1950s norms. But by 1968 Japanese car production exceeded domestic market requirements, and the country's car manufacturers made a determined attack on export markets. Britain was one of their targets.

So, during the 1970s, the names of Colt, Datsun, Honda, Mazda and Toyota entered the consciousness of car-buying families. Colt was actually the

Move up to a Colt

Mitsubishi cars were initially brought into Britain by the Colt Car Company and were marketed as Colts. The suggestion on this sales brochure that they might be aspirational was not generally borne out in practice, but they were reliable.

105 mph Colt Celeste

105 mph Colt Galant

100 mph Colt Lancer

99 mph Colt Galant Estate

A tough new breed of car

COLT

From the Mitsubishi Motor Corporation

The Colt Car Co., Ltd. Dollar Street House, Dollar St., Cirencester, Glos. Tel: 5270

This Colt advertisement promoted high top speeds as a Colt characteristic. The Colt Lancer (here in red) and the Galant estate would have appealed to family buyers.

importer's name, and the cars were built by Mitsubishi; Datsun was the name applied to Nissan cars. Most Japanese family cars in this period were rather ordinary but their success was attributable to three main factors: keen pricing, decent equipment levels, and utter reliability. Success in Britain was so rapid that the British government had to persuade the Japanese makers to make a 'voluntary' agreement in order to protect the domestic industry. So for many years the Japanese makers were held back by import quotas that restricted their total share of the British car market to 11 per cent.

In a 1985 retrospective, *Motor* magazine argued:

> For much of the Seventies, the success of Japan's burgeoning motor industry was based as much on conservative plagiarism as on sound quality and high productivity... To the average owner, less interested in dynamics than dependability, [Japanese cars] represented good value for money. Most of them also reflected Japanese characteristics: they were very easy to drive with light steering and idiot-proof gearchanging... [Yet] for all their popularity, very few Japanese imports ... in the Seventies were paragons of design. Humdrum shapes were frequently tarted with fussy decoration, running gear was often on the wrong side of backward. Aesthetically and technically, the Japs fought a rearguard action.

Nissan sold its cars in Britain as Datsuns during the 1970s. This is a Cherry 100A in its 1973 coupé form: simple but reliable, it was the best-looking of the E10 range, which included four-door saloons and estates as well.

For all that, a few Japanese cars did stand out in the 1970s. Many people who learned to drive in that decade did so in a Datsun Cherry; in 1975 the Datsun Sunny became the first Japanese car to make the top ten best-sellers' list (with 28,000 sales); and the little Honda Civic and its larger Accord stable-mate won many fans for their affordable practicality and dependability.

There were three generations of Cherry in the 1970s, the 100A (1970–4), the F10 (1974–8), and the N10 (1978–82). They were all distinctively styled – the first-generation car especially so, with its upswept rear side window and thick rear pillars, which tended to make the estate version look like an ineptly converted van. It was simply engineered, despite its front-wheel drive (Datsun's first), and lasted as long as its first owners wanted, even if long-term durability was less impressive. The second-generation cars were slightly larger, with more

cabin room and, although there were four-doors and coupés as well, most sales in Britain were of the two-door saloon. The later Cherrys brought no real mechanical advances, but benefited from a slick restyle in a more obviously European idiom, as their makers gained a clearer understanding of what buyers wanted.

There were three generations of the Datsun Sunny, too. New in 1970 was the B110 model, which was actually the second car to use the name. It was squarely in the lower-medium mould of the Vauxhall Viva or Hillman Avenger, but with oddly rounded styling, and outrageously showy hubcaps in the Japanese idiom. Simple but ordinary with rear-wheel drive, it came with two or four doors, as saloon, estate or coupé, and it firmly established the Sunny name in Britain.

From 1973 to 1977 the Sunny was a 120Y model, mechanically largely unchanged, but bigger, with more space inside, and again available with a variety of body configurations. The hubcaps, with their plain centres and perforated outer rims, were again a shock to British tastes, but the cars were well finished and sold as fast as their importers could get them into the showrooms. Though the ride could be bumpy and the brakes needed power assistance, they had a good gearchange allied to oddly spaced gear ratios and a whining gearbox. They gave way in 1977 to a rebodied Sunny, still called 120Y, and still with strangely styled hubcaps. There was nothing remotely adventurous about the cars, but they sold even better than their predecessors, to the tune of thirty thousand and more every year in Britain.

Honda's reputation rested on its motorcycles and mopeds, and the first cars it had sold in Britain were miniature economy models that few buyers took seriously. But from 1972 there was the Civic, a 'supermini' with front-wheel drive, transverse engine, disc brakes at the front, and the option of an automatic gearbox as well. It may have been a 'little old lady's car', but that was no insult: it was easy to drive, affordable and reliable, and later models had the benefit of a hatchback as well. It was a 'sensible' choice for small families. The Accord, introduced in 1976 as a coupé, shared most of the same mechanical elements and had a strong appeal to older buyers, even before a companion four-door model arrived in 1979. Owners liked its equipment levels and quality finish – and, of course, its dependability and low running costs.

The Sunny B110 was a family favourite from 1970 to 1973. This battered example has lost its individualistic wheel trims, but would probably keep going regardless – which was why these simple Japanese saloons sold so well.

APPENDIX

By 1973, many of the old models carried over from the 1960s had gone out of production, and the new cars of the 1970s were on sale. In April that year, the price ceiling for family cars was informally understood to be £1,500, inclusive of Special Car Tax and VAT. The prices shown in the following two lists are rounded to the nearest pound and are for typical family choices within the relevant model ranges. These were not necessarily the cheapest version of each type. Automatic gearboxes and estate models invariably cost extra.

British Leyland	Austin 1100 4-door Super	£929
	Austin Maxi 1500	£1,182
	Austin 1800	£1,279
	Mini 1000	£784
Citroën	Dyane 4	£715
	GS Club	£1,347
DAF	66 Luxe	£1,079
Datsun	100A 4-door	£968
	1200 4-door	£1,028
	160B	£1,289
Fiat	127 3-door	£963
	124	£1,147
Ford	Escort 1300L 4-door	£1,014
	Cortina 1600 4-door	£1,092
	Consul 2000	£1,360
Hillman	Imp	£683
	Avenger 4-door	£909
	Hunter DL	£1,037
Humber	Sceptre	£1,475
Mazda	1300	£1,105
Morris	Marina 1.3	£944
	1800	£1,279
Moskvich	412	£717
Opel	Kadett 4-door	£1,046
	Ascona 1.6	£1,467
Peugeot	304	£1,363

Renault	4DL	£798
	5TL	£956
	12TL	£1,117
	16TL	£1,311
Saab	96 (V4)	£1,302
Simca	1100LS 5-door	£971
Skoda	S100L	£796
Toyota	Corolla 1200	£1,115
Triumph	Toledo 4-door	£1,039
Vauxhall	Viva SL 4-door	£1,119
	Victor 2300SL	£1,413
Volkswagen	1200 'Beetle'	£885
Wartburg	Knight	£760

By the end of the 1970s, inflation had taken its toll on the cost of family saloons, and the price ceiling was around £5,000, again inclusive of Special Car Tax and VAT. The prices shown below are from December 1979 and have been rounded to the nearest pound.

Alfa Romeo	Alfasud 1.3 Super	£3,620
British Leyland	Austin Allegro 1.3 4-door	£3,330
	Austin Maxi 1500	£4,093
	Mini Clubman	£3,000
Morris	Marina 1.3L 4-door	£3,694
	Princess 1700HL	£4,694
Citroen	2CV6	£2,072
	GS Club	£3,633
Colt	Sigma 1600GL	£4,509
Datsun	Sunny 1.2 GLS 4-door	£3,363
	Bluebird 160B	£3,990
Fiat	127L 3-door	£2,821
	Mirafiori 1300L 4-door	£3,554
Ford	Fiesta 1.1S	£3,648
	Escort 1300GL 4-door	£3,700
	Cortina 1600GL	£4,588
Honda	Civic 1200 5-door	£3,150
	Accord 4-door	£4,350
Lada	1200	£2,280
Opel	Kadett GL 4-door	£4,141
	Ascona 1.6 4-door	£3,934

Peugeot	104GL	£2,999
	305GL	£3,799
	504	£4,616
Renault	4TL	£2,848
	5TL	£3,218
	12TL	£3,693
Skoda	105S	£1,970
Talbot	Sunbeam 1300GL	£3,476
	Horizon GL	£3,801
	Avenger 1300GL 4-door	£3,794
	Alpine GL	£4,288
	2-litre	£4,966
Toyota	Starlet 5-door	£3,141
	Corolla 1200 4-door	£3,128
Triumph	Dolomite 1300	£3,832
Vauxhall	Chevette L 4-door	£3,335
	Viva L 4-door	£3,273
	Cavalier 1600L 4-door	£3,989
Volkswagen	Polo L	£3,245
	Golf L 5-door	£3,699
	Passat LS	£4,783
Volvo	343DL	£3,964

BRITISH REGISTRATION NUMBER SUFFIXES, 1970–9

In the 1970s, the British vehicle registration system used a suffix letter to identify the period in which a vehicle was first registered. The 'year' ran from August to July, at the request of the car manufacturers, who recognised the benefit to sales of a new suffix letter at a time when they were trying to clear old stock from the showrooms. Some cars of course carry 'private' or 'cherished' numbers, for which owners pay extra, and which may be impossible to date easily. A typical number would read ABC 123H (dating from 1969–70).

SUFFIXES

H	1969–70		P	1975–6
J	1970–1		R	1976–7
K	1971–2		S	1977–8
L	1972–3		T	1978–9
M	1973–4		V	1979–80
N	1974–5			

PLACES TO VISIT

Beaulieu National Motoring Museum, Beaulieu, New Forest, Hampshire
SO42 7ZN. Telephone: 01590 612345. Website: www.beaulieu.co.uk
Cotswold Motoring Museum & Toy Collection, The Old Mill, Bourton-on-the-
Water, Gloucestershire, GL54 2BY. Telephone: 01451 821255.
Website: www.cotswoldmotoringmuseum.co.uk
Coventy Transport Museum, Millennium Place, Hales Street, Coventry CV1 1JD.
Telephone: 024 7623 4270. Website: www.transport-museum.com
Heritage Motor Centre, Banbury Road, Gaydon, Warwickshire, CV35 0BJ.
Telephone: 01926 641188. Website: www.heritage-motor-centre.co.uk
Haynes International Motor Museum, Sparkford, Yeovil, Somerset, BA22 7LH.
Telephone: 01963 440 804. Website: www.haynesmotormuseum.com
The Heritage Motor Centre, Banbury Road, Gaydon, Warwickshire CV35 0BJ.
Telephone: 01926 641188. Website: www.heritage-motor-centre.co.uk
The home of the Heritage Collection and the British Motor Industry
Heritage Trust houses a representative collection of cars of the 1970s
and 1980s. The collection is rotated from time to time, and not every
vehicle is always on display.
Lakeland Motor Museum, Old Blue Mill, Kendal Road, Backbarrow,
Cumbria LA12 8TA. Telephone: 015395 30400.
Website: www.lakelandmotormuseum.co.uk

FURTHER READING

In a book of this size, it has not been possible to mention every single
model of family car that was available in Britain during the 1970s. So for
those who are interested in finding out more, the following books are
recommended reading.

Georgano, G. N. *Cars of the Seventies and Eighties*. Park Lane, 1990.
Robson, Graham. *A-Z of Cars of the 1970s*. Bay View Books, 1990.
Ruppert, James. *The British Car Industry – Our Part in Its Downfall*. Foresight
Publications, 2008.

INDEX